an infatuations notebook

# Astrology

by Tim Goodwin

Illustrations by Sarah Young

Cover artwork Gordon Parker

Museum Quilts

9/21/00   Dr. Mervin Warren
Rom 13: 11, 12
Titus 2:13

Aries, 21 March – 20 April
Aries, the first sign of the Zodiac, reigns from 21 March
to 20 April and is the sign of the Pioneer. A typical Aries
is slim, with a strong body, thick shoulders, long neck
and luxuriant hair.

Helena: Monsieur Parolles, you were born under a
charitable star.
Parolles: Under Mars, I.
H: I especially think, under Mars.
P: Why under Mars?
H: The wars have so kept you under that you must needs
be born under Mars.
P: When he was predominant.
H: When he was retrograde, I think rather.
P: Why think you so?
H: You go so much backward when you fight.
William Shakespeare, *All's Well That Ends Well*

The ruler of Aries is Mars. Mars is the planet of virility
and procreative powers, the active male force. Mars
usually encourages bravery, energy and stamina, though
also selfishness and aggressiveness.

For a breeze of morning moves
And the planet of Love is on high,
Beginning to faint in the light that she loves
On a bed of daffodil sky.
Alfred Tennyson, *Maud*, 1855

Aries people need partners, without them they are often too selfish. Their impulsiveness often leads to infidelities, and the excitement usually lies in the chase, not the conquest.

'When we wanted to give our sister as wife to Bernard
Clergue, we went to see Guillaume Authié the heretic to
ask his advice on the following question: "when will the
moon be propitious to marry our sister to Bernard?"
Guillaume Authié told us to fix the wedding on a day
which he indicated to us. And so we did.'
Inquisition Register of Jacques Fournier, *c.*1318–25

Circulus meridianus.
Fir ma nic fú
Saturn.
Iuppit.
Mars
Sol.
Ven.
Mercur.
Luna
Horizon obliquus
Aequino
Tropic
Zodiacus
VRANIA
ORONTIVS.

Taurus, 21 April–21 May

Taurus, the second sign of the Zodiac which rules from 21 April to 21 May, is the sign of Love and Possession. Taureans are usually short and well-set, with broad hands, heavy eyebrows and fine profiles. Women are often exceptionally beautiful.

Natives of Taurus, especially women, are often very attractive and are rich in sex appeal. Their sex lives are likely to have a voluptuous, natural intensity. Nakedness is considered natural and wholesome.

Those born in Taurus are generally robust and stoical faced with pain, but are in danger of becoming overweight. Taureans often sing well, but the throat is a weak spot and needs looking after.

Taureans are keen to accumulate personal possessions and money. They are determined, even obstinate, and may be lazy, slow to anger, but fierce when roused. They work hard, have artistic tastes, but are essentially down-to-earth.

'Bring in our daughter, clothed like a bride,
For the embracements even of Jove himself;
At whose conception, till Lucina reigned,
Nature this dowry gave, to glad her presence,
The senate-house of planets all did sit,
To knit in her their best perfections.'
William Shakespeare, *Pericles*, *c*.1608

Gemini, 22 May–21 June
Gemini, the third sign of the Zodiac, covers the time 22
May to 21 June, and is the sign of Mental Activity. The
typical Gemini look is tall and upright, slender, with
artistic hands and restless gestures.

Natives of Gemini are talkative (telephone bills can be huge!), flexible and interested in many different things. They may be extravagant and usually have fine hand-eye co-ordination, will try anything once, but suffer from a lack of tenacity.

TERRÆ·MO·TVS

The love lives of those born in Gemini will probably be varied as they are wandering in their affections and often love more than one person at the same time. They tend to leave marriage as an open question for a considerable time.

Natives of Gemini are prone to coughs and colds. But
their worst problems often stem from congenital
restlessness and inability to relax. Nevertheless they
also come from the most youthful of all signs, physically
and mentally.

'You will not seek to be any lord's astrologer; you will
not exercise any forbidden art for anyone; you will not
choose times (by astrology) for journeys or blood-
letting...you will not waste time in geometry, arithmetic,
rhetoric, judicial astrology, etc, which are arts reproved
by Seneca, and are much more to be rejected by a
spiritual man or a Christian.'
Gerhard Groote, *c.*1374

Cancer, 22 June–22 July

Cancer is the fourth sign of the Zodiac and rules from 22 June to 22 July. It is the sign of Home and Maternal Love. Natives of Cancer are likely to have expressive faces, hips slimmer than their chests, and a tendency to plumpness.

Cancerians traditionally don't much like exercise, and are likely to focus on the arts or consumer affairs. They work hard, aim to make money, enjoy responsibility, and are possessive and domesticated.

Cancer is dominated by the Moon, which represents
receptiveness — the subconscious, emotions, instincts,
the Soul. Traditionally the Moon dominates agriculture
and everything to do with fertility, as well as family life.

The shy, cautious Cancerian is likely to marry for security more than love, and home will always mean more than sex. Generally they want a nice simple sex life.

'Flavia's a wit, has too much sense to pray;
To toast our wants and wishes is her way;
Nor asks of God, but of her stars, to give
The mighty blessing, "while we live, to live".'
Alexander Pope, *Moral Essays*, 1732

Leo, 23 July–22 August
The fifth sign of the Zodiac, from 23 July to 22 August, is Leo, the sign of the vital Love Force. People born under Leo usually have broad shoulders and good legs. Eyes are blue, grey, or dark amber. The complexion is often ruddy.

Leos are proud, charismatic, dignified and commanding
— born leaders. They are generous, but can be conceited,
or very reserved. All Leos have a strong sense of humour
and many like practical jokes.

Leo is governed by the Sun, the giver of life, which represents creativity and health. The Sun vitalises all the other planets, for without it there would be no life anywhere.

To be born in Leo generally means happiness in marriage, and fertility and children are strong in this sign. Boy children bear a striking resemblance to their mother. Leos are unrestrained lovers, but can have problems.

'Tempt not the stars, young man, thou canst not play
With the severity of fate.'
John Ford, *The Broken Heart*, 1633

Virgo, 23 August–22 September
Virgo, the sixth sign of the Zodiac, is the sign of Service and rules from 23 August to 22 September. The typical look of a Virgo is neat, well-groomed and pleasantly precise, sometimes with a pointed chin. They often like floral patterns.

Virgos often allow others to outshine them, and their self-expression may develop late in life. They have good memories, a strong work ethic, and enjoy detail. The one thing they will not allow is for others to interfere with their way of work. They are usually their own hardest critics.

Natives of Virgo do not demonstrate the affection they
feel, but are very self-controlled and are often,
inaccurately, described as cold. In fact they are inwardly
very romantic, and may fall secretly in love without
letting anyone know. They only enjoy love-making with
someone they trust, and chastity is strong in this sign.

Virgo is controlled by Mercury. The various gods who symbolised Mercury in different cultures shared wisdom, speed and fluent speech. Its position in the horoscope indicates wit, persuasiveness, aptitude at public speaking, and restlessness. It also governs Gemini.

Those born under Virgo usually take great care of themselves. They often suffer from minor stomach ailments, sometimes due to worry, and sometimes also allergies that grow from the wrong diet.

'Why, man, he doth bestride the narrow world
Like a Colossus; and we petty men
Walk under his huge legs, and peep about
To find ourselves dishonourable graves.
Men at some time are masters of their fates:
The fault, dear Brutus, is not in our stars,
But in ourselves, that we are underlings.'
William Shakespeare, *Julius Caesar*, c.1599

Libra, 23 September–23 October
Libra governs from 23 September to 23 October. It is the seventh sign of the Zodiac, the sign of Partnership and Comparison. The features of Librans are classical with straight noses, fine eyes and hair, and beauty of face and figure alike. The skin is often unusually delicate.

Librans are very diplomatic and good at judging situations. They rarely do anything on their own, but like opinions and advice from others. They have a strong sense of right and wrong, but hate arguments and criticism, and can be moody.

Love can be a very important part of the life of Librans, and they are often captivating and very popular. Although they do not seem to be assertive, they nearly always get their own way in the end, while appearing to give way. This can especially apply to getting the person they wish to marry. Librans are fascinated by sex, but often rather insecure about it.

After Cosimo de Medici's death in 1464, the praises
heaped on him by his friend Vespasiano da Bisticci
included the fact that 'astrologers found him well versed
in their science, for he had a certain faith in astrology,
and employed it to guide him on certain private
occasions'.

Scorpio, 24 October–22 November
Scorpio, the eighth sign of the Zodiac, is the sign of
Occult Force and also Regeneration. It rules from 24
October to 22 November. Scorpios are usually dark,
with powerful, square-set bodies, and of medium height.
The hair is dark and curly, the eyes fascinating.

Scorpios are strong and silent, with enormous will-power and great personal magnetism. They are intense, untiring, persistent, and rarely fail in their aims.
They have long memories for good and bad, can be rather pleased with themselves, and are sometimes unpleasantly sarcastic.

Scorpio used to be governed by Mars, but after the discovery of Pluto in 1930, it was given to Pluto, as both sign and planet share underworld connections. Pluto is the planet of inner experiences.

A stable relationship is crucial to Scorpios. They are very
demonstrative, and of all the signs, they show the
greatest interest in sex, but can also be very jealous.

'Does the fish soar to find the ocean,
The eagle plunge to find the air –
That we ask of the stars in motion
If they have rumour of thee there.'
Francis Thompson, *The Kingdom of God*, 1859-1907

Sagittarius, 23 November–22 December
Sagittarius is the ninth sign of the Zodiac and rules from
23 November to 22 December. It is the sign of high Aim
to Self-development. Sagittarians are tall and may
develop a slight stoop. They sometimes look rather
aristocratic, but they are always informal and their
general expression is one of laughter and enthusiasm.

Sagittarians are open, optimistic, independent and impulsive, but can get rather pleased with themselves. They have very high principles, talk quickly and are careless of their belongings, often losing them. They are also the great travellers of the Zodiac, preferring the journey itself to arrival.

Sagittarius is ruled by Jupiter, the planet that represents earthly experience conquered by the Soul, and thus, impartiality, judgement and authority. The dominant male god Jupiter is a sign of good luck, and material success, though sometimes also gluttony and self-indulgence.

Marriage is necessary to natives of Sagittarius and very often they marry twice. They take chances on love and enter relationships recklessly. Once in them they are very warm and physical and enjoy a lot of hugging and cuddling.

'What? Think you so many thousand stars shine on in vain? What else, indeed, is it which causes those skilled in nativities to err than that they assign us to a few stars, although all those that are above us have a share in the control of our fate?...But even those stars that are motionless, or because of their speed keep equal pace with the rest of the universe and seem not to move, are not without rule and dominion over us.'
Seneca, c.50

Capricorn, 23 December–20 January
Capricorn, the tenth sign of the Zodiac, is the sign of
patience and reliability. It rules from 23 December to 20
January. Capricorns are usually serious and restrained in
looks, and are often small with good legs. They wear
dark clothes, and may look older than they are.

Capricorns are patient and reliable, but behind their reserve lies fierce ambition. They take status very seriously, as they do most things, and are willing to work hard to achieve their aims. Security is important to them.

AN IMV S
SVBIMAGINE.
INCVBVIT.
ALTIOR
MVNDO
Astrologia
Ptolomeus

The planet that rules Capricorn is Saturn. Saturn is
Father Time, Santa Claus, and represents teaching,
responsibility and duty, but can also be the bringer
of sorrows.

Women born in Capricorn often delay marrying until quite late, marry older partners, or do not marry at all. Capricorns can be the finest of all lovers and work just as hard for their partners as themselves.

Capricorns can be weak when they are young, but grow tougher and are frequently very long-lived. Things to watch for are rheumatism, and skin and teeth problems.

Aquarius, 21 January–19 February
Aquarius covers the period from 21 January to 19
February. It is the eleventh sign of the Zodiac, and the
sign of Humanitarian Interest and Strong Will. Aquarian
women have broad shoulders, large bones, and a long
neck. They dress dramatically and unconventionally. The
typical Aquarius man is usually taller than average,
strongly built with a high broad forehead and a
distinctive profile.

Aquarians spend a lot of time worrying about other people. They are good judges of people, sincere, cheerful, original, emotional, and sometimes timid, but their opinions are not easily changed. Freedom is very important to them, both in practice and theory.

On Friday 12 January 1996 Uranus moved into Aquarius and a new age arrived, many years after the musical *Hair* proclaimed 'This is the dawning of the Age of Aquarius.' Having taken two thousand years to arrive, it may be another two or three centuries before the Age of Aquarius is fully established. It is expected to be a time of liberality, cosmopolitanism, anti-discrimination, and the questioning of inherited power and money.

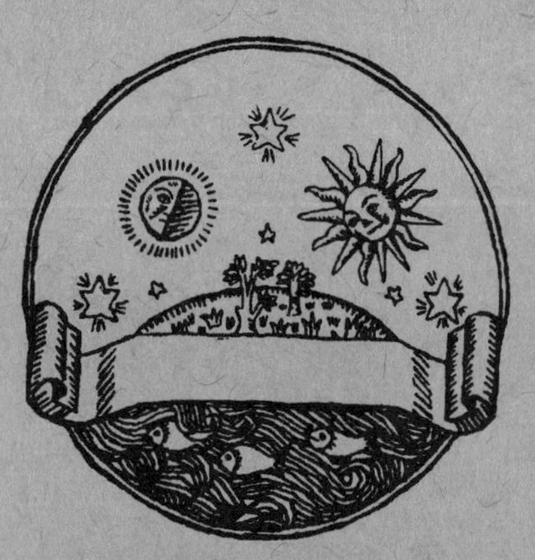

Aquarius was originally ruled by Saturn, but the discovery of Uranus in 1781 led to the sign being changed over. Uranus is considered the planet of intuition, of pioneers and the divine rebel.

Aquarians seek for ideal lovers, and are usually slow to make advances. They are very faithful and often marry someone of opposite tastes to themselves. Aquarians are likely to be very assiduous about hygiene and contraception, and are rarely jealous.

Pisces, 20 February–March 20

Pisces, the twelfth and last sign of the Zodiac, rules from 20 February to 20 March, and is the sign of Resignation and Adaptation. Pisceans are usually shorter than average with a faintly clumsy air about them, and sometimes look a bit of a mess. They have warm smiles, and good skin, but may not look particularly healthy.

Those born in Pisces tend to accept things as they are rather than try to change them. They are sympathetic, giving people, who always see the best in everyone, which can lead them to make mistakes. Their strong characters specially come to the fore when looking after family and friends.

In love and marriage Pisceans are affectionate but changeable and frequently marry twice. There are often several children, but some Pisceans choose platonic unions. Pisces natives are usually more interested in romance than physical love-making.

A Signis coeli nolite metuere. REX

Somewhere around the birth of Jesus Christ the earth
slipped into the Age of Pisces. It has ruled ever since,
though now its ascendancy is finally over. It was
variously described as the age of brotherly love, and of
the Saviour — with everyone looking for someone to
teach what was right and wrong.

'Behold, there came wise men from the east to Jerusalem, saying "where is he that is born King of the Jews? For we have seen his star in the east, and are come to worship him"... Then Herod, when he had privily called the wise men, inquired of them diligently what time the star appeared. And he sent them to Bethlehem, and so, "Go and search diligently for the young child; and when ye have found him, bring me word again, that I may come and worship him also."'
*Matthew*, 2, 1-8

'The seductiveness of astrology lies in its pretension to combine a theory which explains the whole machina mundi with a practice which will enable Tom, Dick and Harry to spot the Derby winner now.'
Arnold Toynbee, 1946

The sun enters each sign of the Zodiac at a different time, and even a different date, each year. If you are born close to the changeover dates, it is called being on the cusp. This does not usually mean that you are a mixture of both signs, only that which sign you are depends on which year you were born.

'We are merely the stars' tennis-balls, struck and
        bandied
Which way please them.'
John Webster, *The Duchess of Malfi*, 1614

Birthstones: Aries – Diamond; Taurus – Emerald; Gemini – Garnet; Cancer – Pearl; Leo – Ruby; Virgo – Agate, Onyx; Libra – Sapphire, Opal; Scorpio – Topaz; Sagittarius – Turquoise; Capricorn – Jet; Aquarius – Amethyst, Aquamarine; Pisces – Bloodstone.

Those born in Aries should get on well with those born in Sagittarius or Leo. Gemini and Aquarius are good also, but they should beware of Cancer, Capricorn and Libra.

Virgo and Capricorn make good partners for
Taureans. Cancer and Pisces are suitable too, but
not Leo or Aquarius.

Gemini goes well with Libra, Aquarius, Aries and Leo, but not with Sagittarius, Virgo or Pisces.

Cancer should look for partners in Pisces or Scorpio. They also get on well with Virgo and Taurus, but Capricorn, Aries and Libra are too strong to be compatible.

Aries and Sagittarius are the best partners for natives of Leo. Gemini and Virgo are good too. They should steer clear of Taurus and Aquarius.

Virgo gets on best with Capricorn and Taurus, and also Scorpio and Cancer. Gemini and Pisces are unlikely to be suitable.

Aquarius and Gemini go well with Libra, especially the former. Leo and Sagittarius also show empathy, but not Aries or Cancer.

Pisces and Cancer work well with Scorpio, as do Virgo
and Capricorn, but not Aquarius.

Sagittarians should choose their partners from Leo and Aries, or possibly Libra and Aquarius, but not Gemini or Pisces.

The ideal partners for Capricorn are those with birthdays close to the same date in May or September. The months of March and November also go well. Partners born in April, July or October are likely to create friction.

Aquarius goes best with Gemini, which counteracts Aquarian lethargy, or Libra. Aries and Sagittarius combine well also, but not Scorpio or Taurus, and especially not Leo.

Pisces goes well with Cancer or Scorpio, and also suits
Taurus and Capricorn. They should steer clear of
Sagittarius, Gemini and Virgo.

Sympathetic creatures: Aries – sheep, lambs; Taurus – cattle; Gemini – small birds, especially doves; Cancer – crabs, tortoises and turtles; Leo – big cats; Virgo – domestic pets especially dogs; Libra – small creatures; Scorpio – reptiles; Sagittarius – horses; Capricorn – goats and donkeys; Aquarius – large birds, especially eagles; Pisces – fish, dolphins and whales.

'Sire,' he said. 'You know how long I have lived and studied the stars; for we Centaurs live longer than you Men, and even longer than your kind, Unicorn. Never in all my days have I seen such terrible things written in the skies as there have been nightly since this year began. The stars say nothing of the coming of Aslan, nor of peace, nor of joy. I know by my art there have not been such disastrous conjunctions of the planets for five hundred years. It was already in my mind to come and warn Your Majesty that some great evil hangs over Narnia. But last night the rumour reached me that Aslan is abroad in Narnia. Sire, do not believe this tale. It cannot be. The stars never lie, but Men and Beasts do.'
C S Lewis, *The Last Battle*, 1956

Denmark, England, and Germany are governed by Aries.
Famous people born under Aries include Marlon
Brando, Casanova, Diana Ross, and Leonardo da Vinci.

Iran, Ireland, Switzerland, and the Greek Islands are governed by Taurus. Famous Taureans include Cher, Queen Elizabeth II, Sigmund Freud, and William Shakespeare.

Belgium, USA and Wales are governed by Gemini.
Famous Geminis include Bob Dylan, John F Kennedy,
Marilyn Monroe and Queen Victoria.

Netherlands, New Zealand and Scotland are governed
by Cancer. Celebrated natives of Cancer include
Louis Armstrong, Princess Diana, Rembrandt, and
Jean-Paul Sartre.

The Czech Republic, France, especially the South, Italy and Rumania are governed by Leo. Famous Leos include Napoleon Bonaparte, Mick Jagger, Jacqueline Kennedy-Onassis, and Robert Redford.

Brazil, Greece, Turkey and the West Indies are governed
by Virgo. Celebrated Virgos include Sean Connery,
Greta Garbo, D H Lawrence, and Twiggy.

Austria, China, Japan, and Canada are governed by
Libra. Well-known Librans include Mahatma Gandhi,
Bob Geldof, John Lennon and Oscar Wilde.

Morocco and Norway are ruled by Scorpio. Famous Scorpios include Prince Charles, Marie Curie, Indira Gandhi, and Pablo Picasso.

Australia, South Africa and Spain are ruled by Sagittarius. Famous Sagittarians include Jane Austen, Winston Churchill, Walt Disney, and Jimi Hendrix.

India and Mexico are ruled by Capricorn. Famous
Capricorns include Marlene Dietrich, Howard Hughes,
Joan of Arc, and Martin Luther King.

Poland, Russia, and Sweden are ruled by Aquarius.
Famous Aquarians include Mozart, Ronald Reagan,
Vanessa Redgrave, and Virginia Woolf.

Finland and Portugal are ruled by Pisces. Famous
Pisceans include Albert Einstein, Michelangelo, Rudolf
Nureyev, and Elizabeth Taylor.

The three most important elements of a birth-chart are the Sun-sign which comes from the date on which you are born; the Rising-sign, which depends on the time and place you were born; and the Moon-sign, the moon taking about two and a half days to travel through each sign of the zodiac.

Louis of Orleans, brother of King Charles VI, had his own astrologers, as did virtually all of the French nobility of the time who could afford it. After Louis was murdered in 1407, Jean Petit, a doctor of the University of Paris, publicly justified his murder partly because of Louis' dabblings in the occult. However Petit himself was well-known for his powers of prophecy.

Lucky plants: Aries – thistle; Taurus – daisy;
Gemini – orchid, lily-of-the-valley; Cancer – lotus;
Leo – sunflower, marigold; Virgo – narcissus, forget-me-not; Libra – rose, strawberry; Scorpio – blackthorn;
Sagittarius – oak; Capricorn – ivy, yew;
Aquarius – myrrh, rue; Pisces – water lily.

The new-born child, up to the age of four, is ruled by the Moon. Children from five to fourteen are governed by Mercury, then comes the third age during which Venus is dominant. The prime of life, from twenty-three to forty-one, is ruled by the Sun. The fifth age, from forty-two to fifty-six belongs to Mars; fifty-seven to sixty-eight is the age of Jupiter; while from sixty-eight to death, the seventh and final age, is the realm of Saturn.

Aries, Leo, and Sagittarius are Fire signs. Taurus, Virgo and Capricorn are Earth signs. Gemini, Libra and Aquarius are Air signs. Cancer, Pisces and Scorpio are Water signs. Earth and Water represent the female signs.

During the first-ever circumnavigation of the globe Ferdinand Magellan lost contact with one of his ships, the *San Antonio*. After searching and failing to find it, he asked the astrologer on his own ship what had happened. The astrologer plotted the stars, consulted his books, and told Magellan that there had been a mutiny and the *San Antonio* had sailed back to Spain, which it eventually turned out was precisely what had happened.

The Chinese Emperor employed a hereditary Imperial Astrologer. His job was to watch the movements of the planets and stars, and work out the good and bad fortune they implied. All parts of the empire were connected with specific stars, and he also used the winds and clouds to help him. His prophecies were top secret, and it was strictly against the law to reveal them to the common people.

'There was no art with which to foresee things to come, but men's conjectures were a sort of lottery, and out of many things which they said should come to pass, some actually did, unawares to those who spoke it, who stumbled upon it through how much they said.'
Saint Augustine, *Confessions*, 397

Lady Eleanor Davies's anti-royalist prophecies in the 1630s led to her being thrown in prison. After her release she presented the newly-triumphant Oliver Cromwell with a book of prophecies, inscribed, 'Behold he cometh with ten thousand of his saints to execute judgement on all', and contrasting Cromwell as the sun in splendour against the sickly crescent moon of Charles I. Cromwell put on his spectacles, smiled, and remarked, 'But we are not all saints.'

Lucky metals: Aries – iron; Taurus – copper;
Gemini – mercury; Cancer – silver; Leo – gold;
Virgo – nickel, mercury; Libra – bronze, copper;
Scorpio – steel, iron; Sagittarius – tin;
Capricorn – lead, silver; Aquarius – aluminium, lead;
Pisces – platinum, tin.

Natives of Aries are often involved in the armed forces.
Other popular careers include anything to do with travel
or politics, precise scientific work such as engineering
and electronics, and general crafts, including carpentry.

Taurus is the sign for those who work on or with the land, especially farmers. General jobs linked with investment, banking, insurance, and real estate are also popular. Taureans can be excellent cooks.

Those born under Gemini are likely to be drawn to graphics, lecturing, art and music, and anything to do with writing. Scientific research may be popular, as may being an agent or accountant. Selling is a favourite Gemini career also.

Cancer is a good sign for nurses, obstetricians, midwives, gynaecologists and primary and nursery school teachers. Other interests include music (especially stringed instruments), gardening, selling food, the social services, boats and antiques.

Leos are especially suited for the stage. Other careers that appeal include law, politics, teaching, directing, management and any self-employed job. Leos also like to be involved with the sea.

Virgos are excellent personal assistants, and make fine
researchers. They are also at home in medicine, law,
engineering, and criticism.

Librans are at their very best in promoting the talents of others. Jobs that may appeal include public relations and advertising, fashion, diplomacy and the civil service.

There is a wide range of work that Scorpios may be attracted to. Detectives, scientists, insurers and market analysts, members of the navy, researchers, pharmacists and anyone involved with the occult, have a good chance of being Scorpios. Criminals are often born in this sign also.

Sagittarians are usually drawn to the law and religion. They also enjoy working in universities, writing, the clothing trade, working with animals, and there is a higher than average number of professional sportsmen and sportswomen.

Banking and all jobs to do with finance are popular with
Capricorns. Other suitable careers include dentistry,
local government, anything to do with building and
manual labour, and running your own business.

Aquarius is the sign for dancers, artists and workers in the social sciences. Work in television and radio is also popular, as is inventing and work in charity and social services. Work to do with pictures, such as photography and radiography are possible.

Pisces provides the sort of actors who hide their personalities, where Leos parade it. Advertising, public relations, counselling, church work, and jobs in the service industries are all suitable and many Pisceans end up as executives or administrators.

You stars that reigned at my nativity,
Whose influence hath allotted death and hell
Now draw up Faustus like a foggy mist,
Into the entrails of yon labouring cloud,
That when you vomit forth into the air,
My limbs may issue from your smoky mouths,
So that my soul may but ascend to heaven.
Christopher Marlowe, *Doctor Faustus, c.*1588

Lucky colours: Aries – red; Taurus – pastels;
Gemini – yellow; Cancer – grey; Leo – orange;
Virgo – brown; Libra – pink; Scorpio – deep red;
Sagittarius – purple; Capricorn – black;
Aquarius – blue; Pisces – green.

'There are many who do not presume either to bathe, or
to dine, or to appear in public, till they have diligently
consulted, according to the rules of astrology, the
situation of Mercury and the aspect of the moon.'
Ammianus Marcellinus, *c*.380

'When beggars die there are no comets seen;
The heavens themselves blaze forth the death of princes.'
William Shakespeare, *Julius Caesar*, c.1599

When the astronomer and mathematician Edmund
Halley sneered at Isaac Newton's interest in astrology,
Newton retorted, 'Sir, I have studied it, you have not.'

Many of the most famous buildings in Florence were begun on days considered propitious by the astrologers. Before work was started on the biggest historical monument in the city, the Fortezza da Basso, the especially celebrated astrologers of Bologna arrived and chose 15 July 1534 as the day to lay the foundation stone.

At the end of every year, the Aztecs believed came 'five empty days', when fires were put out, fasting was general and work and love-making forbidden. On the dawn of the fifth day the priests, after consulting their astrological calendars and observing the Pleiades rising in the heavens, formally declared the world was not about to end, and fires could be relit from a sacred fire.

In the seventeenth century it was high treason to cast the monarch's horoscope without formal permission.

William Laud, the Archbishop of Canterbury, preached a sermon before Parliament during the reign of Charles I stating that the power of prayer was so great it could even overcome the influence of a malign conjunction or opposition of planets (as there was one then).

'When they had heard the king, they departed; and lo,
the star which they saw in the east, went before them, till
it came and stood over where the young child was. When
they saw the star, they rejoiced with exceeding great joy.'
*Matthew* 2, 9-10

'There is no returning game between a man and his stars.'
Samuel Beckett, *Murphy*, 1938

Published by Museum Quilts (UK) Inc.
254-258 Goswell Road, London EC1V 7EB



EAN: 5 026285 00160 5



Printed and bound in Hong Kong